A Confident Choices Book

You CAN Write a Book!

The No-Nonsense Guide to Self-Publishing

By Julie Beyer, MA

NutraConsults, LLC

You CAN Write a Book: The No-Nonsense Guide to Self-Publishing
A Confident Choices® Book
ISBN: 978-0-9767246-8-1
First Printing – Trade Paperback

Published in the United States of America by:

NutraConsults, LLC
P.O. Box 210086
Auburn Hills, MI 48321
www.NutraConsults.com

To order a copy of this book, please visit:
www.NutraConsults.com

Disclaimer: Confident Choices®, a trademarked division of NutraConsults, LLC, is not an authority on book writing or publishing. No information written or implied in this book, the NutraConsults website, or any resource recommended should be considered advice for any individual or company, but constitutes a general education regarding self-publishing. Please contact your accountant, attorney, and other business consultants regarding any decisions you make regarding the publishing of your book(s).

Trademark notice: This book uses various trademarked names within its text. In the interest of the reader, we are using the trademarked names in an editorial style. In the interest of the trademark holders, we cite their ownership of the trademarks, with no intention of infringement.

Time sensitive materials: At the time of publication, all names, addresses, telephone numbers, email and Web addresses were verified as accurate.

Dedication

This book is dedicated to my incredible grandmothers, Josephine and Margaret, who lived their lives as all women should: with unconditional love, strength, and gracious charity.

I wish I knew more of your stories.

Preface: "Just Tell Me What to Do"

It is easy to feel overwhelmed in this crazy information saturated world. Whether people are trying to navigate medical information for a disease or attempting to sort out publishing options for their first book, many eventually throw up their hands pleading to no one in particular, "Please, just tell me what to do!"

Essentially, people just want quick answers to their questions, simple guidelines to follow, and solid information so that they can be confident about the decisions they are making.

The *Confident Choices*® brand was developed to meet those needs.

Table of Contents

Part One: First Things First

Part Two: Writing Deliberately

Part Three: Bringing Your Book to Life

Appendices

Part One:

First Things First

"Don't wait until everything is just right. It will never be perfect. There will always be challenges, obstacles and less than perfect conditions. So what?

Get started now. With each step you take, you will grow stronger and stronger, more and more skilled, more and more self-confident and more and more successful."

Mark Victor Hansen
America's Ambassador of Possibility

1. Why Self-Publishing IS for You

"When you cannot make up your mind which of two evenly balanced courses of action you should take—choose the bolder."
William Joseph Slim—British army general

The Business of Publishing Has Changed!

This book is all about cheerleading. I want you to write *your* book. I know you dream about publishing a book or you probably wouldn't be reading this. Perhaps you have even written a book and stashed it in your dresser drawer or buried it in some file on your computer because once you wrote it, you weren't sure what to do with it. You may even have sent a proposal or manuscript to a publisher only to face the frustrating realization that the process established by the book publishing industry is extremely difficult if not impossible to navigate. This can be quite maddening, especially when you read some of the stuff the big companies are putting out there and you know you can do better! So, consider me your book publishing coach. I want you to succeed.

How can I be so certain anyone can publish a book? Because advances in technology offer the biggest opportunities in the world of book publishing since the printing press was invented and the monks put down their quills. Just as books don't have to be hand copied over and over anymore, neither do books have to go through the old-fashioned printing processes. Today, the technology for self-publishing books is readily available and so simple to use that anyone can publish and market a book.

Don't get me wrong; even the process of self-publishing can be intimidating. For years I was told, "You should write a book," yet I was quite confused about the route to take. Then I learned the self-publishing process by taking a community education class offered by our local school district. To be honest, the instructor's method just seemed too good to be true so I went to the bookstore and spent $75 on three other books written about self-publishing. Those books, averaging over 400 pages each, just complicated everything; so I prowled the internet looking for even more information.

Can you guess what I found out after all of that research? That the information taught in the community education class really *was* the best way for me to publish a book. I am still puzzled by why the other books were 400 pages long because honestly, it isn't that hard. It doesn't matter if you want to publish a children's book, a self-help book, a book of poetry, a racy novel, or a training manual—the process described in *You CAN Write a Book* is the easiest, fastest, and probably the least expensive way to get your book in print.

The Benefits of Self-Publishing

Of course, easy, fast, and inexpensive aren't the only reasons to self-publish:

1. **You have more creative control throughout the process.** That doesn't mean you *have* to do everything, but if you struggle with turning your work over to others, self-publishing is a great way to keep your hands in the project from beginning to end.
2. **It gives you a chance to start slowly.** With current self-publishing technology, you don't have to fill your basement or garage with 10,000 books that you may or may not sell in your lifetime. Depending on your need or budget you can order as few as 25 books; but keep in mind, the best price breaks begin when you order at least 250 books.
3. **You can update and improve your content easily with each printing.** Use your first printing to get feedback, fix errors, and even change formats. With just a few adjustments, you can even take book from print to e-book, without having to go through the hoops of an online publisher!
4. **You have more financial control.** When you print fewer than five thousand books, using an online publisher is usually cheaper than other methods, and you get to keep more of the profits (see Table 1). You can also decide how much money you want to spend on tasks like cover design, document layout, and editing. If you are competent and creative, you can save a lot of money by doing things yourself!

Table 1: Profit Comparisons of Different Publishing Options
(Example for 1000 books, 180 pages per book)

Type of Printing	$ per book	$ Retail	Profit (Profit per 1000)
Off-set	$13.50	$20.00	$6.50 ($6500)
Kinko's	$11.50	$20.00	$8.50 ($8500)
Online Publisher	$2.75	$20.00	$17.50 ($17,250)

5. **You retain the rights to your book and can parlay it into multiple streams of income.** You wrote the book; why not reap as many benefits as possible? From setting up a webpage to sell your book directly, to selling pieces of it as magazine articles or for content on other websites, you get to decide how you want to nurture your brand identity, selling and often reselling your work.

6. **You can sell your books in online stores like Barnes & Noble and Amazon.com just like any other publisher!** With a little effort you can sell your books in other stores, taking advantage of finely targeted customer audiences.

Minimizing the Risks

Any business venture has its risks. But remember the first rule of business is to make more money than you spend. When you are an author, not only do you want to make money on the physical books themselves, you want to create a semi-passive source of income to make all of your writing efforts worthwhile. (I say semi-passive, because as any author will tell you, as long as you want to sell your book, you will need to actively promote it. Don't worry; we will discuss that in Chapter 9.)

To put it simply, the last thing most of you want to do is put all your time and money into writing and printing a book that isn't going to offer any significant payback. That is why this book guides you through a simple process that can help minimize your costs and efforts while you maximize your profits. For example, in Chapter 3, I illustrate the importance of crafting a finely focused project for a specific target audience. And anyone who does a job wants to make more money per hour of work. That is why Chapter 4 is full of valuable ideas to keep you organized throughout the writing process, effectively minimizing your efforts.

"Writing is an exploration. You start from nothing and learn as you go."

E. L. Doctorow—American Author

Of course, as a self-publisher, you will be doing the writing plus tasks that a traditional publishing company does for its authors. But don't let that curb your enthusiasm for publishing on your own. A lot of that is creative and fun, and there are still ways to maximize your profits, including:

- Crafting your covers and document design to boost the marketing appeal of your book (Chapter 5).
- Streamlining the editing process by doing some of this work yourself, then finding a professional editor who can polish up the final copy (Chapter 6).
- Obtaining your publishing company's International Standard Book Number (ISBN) numbers yourself,

submitting your own book for copyright, and cataloguing your book at an online clearinghouse where anyone can find your book (Chapter 7).

- Using a tried and true online publisher (Chapter 8) and using free and inexpensive methods to advertise and sell your book (Chapter 9).

Of course, nothing is foolproof. There is still the chance that you will end up with boxes of books and no one to buy them. But that can happen with authors who go with traditional publishing too. The way to minimize the risk in any publishing venture is to educate yourself about the process, decide which tasks you are willing (and not willing) to do, and utilize all the technology that is literally at your fingertips.

Key Points of Chapter 1

1. The technology for self-publishing is available for anyone to publish their book.
2. Benefits of self-publishing include:
    a. getting your work to your readers quicker,
    b. controlling every creative and financial aspect of the process,
    c. printing smaller quantities of books for less money than traditional printing processes, and
    d. having the ability to update your manuscript quickly.
3. There are risks when you self-publish your own book; this book will show you how to minimize those risks.

Resources for Chapter 1

Books:

Complete Guide to Self-Publishing: Everything You Need to Know to Write, Publish, Promote, and Sell Your Own Book (Self-Publishing 4th Edition)
By Marilyn and Tom Ross
If you want more information than is offered in *You CAN Write a Book,* you might consider this book. The Ross' not only teach about self-publishing, they go into great detail about selling to a larger publisher, naming your publishing company, designing covers, book pricing, and even where to find lighter-weight shipping envelopes.

Damn! Why Didn't I Write That? How Ordinary People are Raking In $100,000.00...or more Writing Nonfiction Books & How You Can Too!
By Marc McCutcheon
A lighthearted guide encourages capitalizing on publishing niches in order to generate consistent income year after year. The most valuable parts of McCutcheon's book are the stories he tells about dozens of successful authors who have self-published their books. You will find pages of motivation in this book that will keep you moving even when you feel discouraged about your progress with your own book.

Dan Poynter's Self-Publishing Manual, Volume 2: How to Write, Print and Sell Your Own Book

By Dan Poynter

Dan Poynter is considered by many to be the guru of self-publishing. This sequel to the best selling *Self-Publishing Manual* describes how to use new techniques to write your book even faster, use new technology to publish it for less, and how to use social media for promotion.

The Well-Fed Self-Publisher: How to Turn One Book into a Full-Time Living

By Peter Bowerman

Peter Bowman is the king of parlaying the written work into as many versions as possible to maximize your income-to-efforts ratio. Bowerman clearly knows how to integrate creativity with the discipline of task stating, "Success as a self-publisher is far more a function of a process than an aptitude. It's far less about some way you have to be than it is about a bunch of things you have to do."

Websites

Guerrilla Press

www.guerrilla-press.com

This website provides a great overview of various publishing methods. Bookmark it for future reference!

Writer's Digest

www.writersdigest.com

With a tag line of "Write Better, Get Published" Writer's Digest offers tips for writers, publishes articles, provides online workshops, and advertises conferences for writers. You can also view blogs and participate in various competitions throughout the year.

2. Assessing Readiness

"Continuous effort—not strength or intelligence—
is the key to unlocking our potential."
Winston Churchill—Past Prime Minister of Great Britain

Equipment and Software

Thirty years ago, authors could not have imagined that today most people have the basic tools they need to publish a book right in their own office or home. Think about how far we have come. It was only fifteen years ago that my family got its first desktop computer. We had a lousy printer back then, and honestly, we played more games on it than anything else!

Five years later we cautiously connected to the online world via an agonizingly slow phone line. Even then, for a family of five, we only had one machine and it became a daily event for one person or another to bargain with the rest for more computer time.

Fast forward another ten years and as our children went to college they each got their own laptop. We also have wireless high speed internet service, webcams, DVD recorders, and even a wireless printer. Not only can I not imagine my world without my gadgets, my livelihood depends on them.

Now, you may or may not be gearing up for a career as a writer, but even the most casual author-publisher needs a few basic tools, or at least know where to borrow them.

Computer. Rather than toss around numbers of GHz or RAM that could be obsolete by this book's second printing, I will simply say it is essential to have a good computer with plenty of processing speed (GHz) and memory (RAM). I have had a hard drive crash when I was working on a large project. It is a nightmare if your files are not backed up. This can happen when your hard drive overheats from running too many programs at once—something you are likely to do if you are writing a book. If you are not sure whether your computer can handle large projects, contact the manufacturer to help you sort things out.

If you are in the market for a new computer, tell the sales agents anything and everything for which you plan on using your computer for. Don't just talk about your book, but also let them know about your work, photos, videos, games, and music. Compare what sales agents from two or more stores say with information you find online, and you should be on your way to making a good decision. **Alternatives:** Most public libraries have computers, although you may need a reservation and be encumbered with time restraints and limited software options. Internet cafes are not as popular as they once were, but they do exist—usually for a steep price.

Software. In the past, self-publishers either had to know how to use or know someone who knew publishing programs such as Quark Express® or Microsoft Publisher®. Today, you can write your book using Microsoft Word® (typically abbreviated as "Word"), the most commonly used word processing program. Word is also compatible with Instant Publisher, the online printing company used in this book.

For files over 90 pages or so, you will probably want to use a program that changes your Word files into a PDF format. Adobe Acrobat is the most common PDF converter program; however several other programs are available, some for free on the internet. I like Adobe Acrobat because I can write and convert one chapter at a time, then combine them into one document at the end. For quick edits, I make changes to the chapter's original Word document, recreate the PDF, then drop the corrected pages into the larger PDF document.

If you are going to put graphics or photos in your book you will definitely need a photo editing program. Most computers that are equipped with the Microsoft Office System have Microsoft Picture Editor, but you can also use a free program available on the internet such as Google's' Picasa. (You can check out Picasa at www.picasa.google.com.)

Do you want to go really high tech with your writing? Try using a voice recognition program. Imagine speaking into a microphone and having your words appear like magic in your Word document. Research your options carefully before you buy anything, however. Many newer computers already have a voice recognition program as a standard feature. These programs also require practice since you have to "train" the computer to recognize your voice and accent. The technology is there, and it is getting better every day.

Printer/scanner. Most of us are not going to actually print our books from our home printer even if it is possible. The ink and paper used in home machines are just too expensive compared to an online printer. However, you *will* want to print out sections of your work occasionally to see how it looks when you hold it in your hands. It is much easier to spot small slips like extra spaces, typos, or grammatical errors in a printed copy. A scanner can be helpful if you want to use your own photos or graphics in your book. And did I mention I *love* my wireless printer? **Alternative:** Once your manuscript is ready for its final review, it is probably cheaper to have the draft printed at an office supply store like OfficeMax® or at a shipping supply center like FedEx Office℠. Their prices are reasonable, you can often email a copy directly to your local center, and they can print the document on both sides, which can be invaluable as you fine tune the look of your finished product.

External storage media. We have already emphasized the importance of having a robust processer and plenty of memory on your computer, but it is just as critical to back up your files apart from of your computer hard drive. There are several sources to consider, each with their pros and cons.

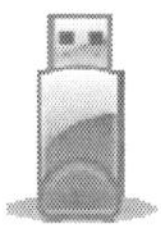

High memory, portable USB drives (also called thumb drives or flash drives) have become the standard for everyday storage of files. They are terrific for transferring your files from computer to computer and transporting your files to a local print center. Some printers can also print from a USB drive. The portability of these drives can also be their downfall, making them more susceptible to theft, loss, or damage. (Hint: Don't keep a portable USB drive in your pockets or you just may put it in the wash!)

CD or DVD burners can also store large files while being very portable. As with USB drives, you can easily transfer files from computer to computer or take your files to a local printer. Most home printers do not accept a CD or DVD for direct printing. Unfortunately, CDs or DVDs are easily scratched or damaged, and may be susceptible to degradation over time. Unlike portable USB drives, however, you probably won't throw a CD in the wash!

External hard drives also use USB ports to connect to your computer but have incredible storage capacity, commonly 500 GB or larger. (As a comparison, most home computers have between 2 and 4 GB.) Although more expensive than flash drives or CD/DVDs, these units are indispensible for storing the information from multiple computers, large amounts of music, and tens of thousands of pictures. After I wrote my second book, I realized I needed more than a collection of flash drives and CDs and spent the $99.00 for substantial peace of mind. If you choose to use an external hard drive, you may want to keep it hooked up to your computer while you are working. I set a timer to go off every 30 minutes or so and not only save my file to my computer but I update the external hard drive.

Internet access. Although you don't need internet access to actually write your book, the internet is rich with help for writers and is a great way to research various topics. Of course, a high speed connection will be a necessity when the time comes to upload your book to Instant Publisher or it could take hours. In my family's case, wireless internet is a necessity. Multiple computers can be connected at the same time with the added benefit of flexibility. I find it helpful to have a change of scenery when I write, moving from my office, to the family room, or into the finished basement in the summer where it is cooler. **Alternatives:** If you do not have internet access or you only have access via a slower connection, consider using a library or internet café computer as mentioned previously. Some libraries have wireless access allowing you to use your personal laptop, or you can visit coffee shops or bookstores that have wireless access. (These locations can also come in handy if you have a power or internet outage!)

Writing Skills

One of the inherent pitfalls of self-publishing is that anyone can publish their book regardless of writing ability. Theoretically, all you have to do is send a document file to Instant Publisher and in turn, they will send you printed copies of your book. No one is going to run a spell check on your work or require that you have someone else edit your work carefully.

Of course, you want to do better than that. You don't want to join the ranks of mediocre writers. You want to write a book to share your ideas with others, but no matter how good your ideas are, you still have something readable. So, if you need some help with the delivery part of your writing, you need to find a way to hone your skills, or find someone else to do the writing for you.

Some of you may already have received feedback on your writing. You know your strengths and weaknesses and know how to leverage them. Others, however, have kept their writing in journals or computer files without showing a soul. If that is true for you, now is the time to get another person's opinion. I don't mean asking your mother or your spouse either. You need someone with enough knowledge of language and writing to provide constructive criticism, because you need to know where you stand. Just as important, you need to be receptive to that sort of help.

In any case, you might find it fun to take a writing class from a local community college or join a local writer's group. I know my writing quickly improved when I went back to school. The feedback that I received from the instructors was priceless and also motivated me to take some risks with my writing. Eventually, I began writing articles for newsletters and doing content for websites and my confidence improved.

If you don't want to go back to school, or you just need some technical help, surround yourself with quality resources to compensate! For example, do you tend to use the same words over and over? Then learn how to use a thesaurus. Microsoft Word even has a built in thesaurus. Just highlight a word and press Shift + F7. A thesaurus window will open to the right of your document displaying a variety of synonyms for the word you chose. Or, if you are unsure about when to use commas, semi-colons, or parentheses, visit the Purdue Online Writing Lab (or OWL). You can even get hints about writing fiction, poetry, technical writing, and revising your work (www.owl.english.purdue.edu).

Personal Characteristics

Certainly, having a passion for writing and possessing a compelling writing style are essential to becoming a successful author, but there is more. We are also talking about acting as your own publisher. Remember, you will not only be writing your book, you will be managing other aspects of the document including design, editing, and the business aspects of the process.

So what other personality traits are essential to success in the self-publishing business?

Motivation to achieve. Are you willing to work hard to achieve your goal? Do you have a track record of taking on difficult tasks and completing them despite unexpected obstacles? Do you find satisfaction in conquering new challenges? If you answered yes to those questions then you have a great start toward success as a self-publisher.

Independent. Only self-starters need apply to be both author and publisher. If you really want to write a book without having an agent or publisher cracking a whip, you must be able to prioritize and schedule your own tasks.

Organized. Even if you are not naturally organized, it is critical to your success to have some system for ordering your ideas, as well as tracking your tasks. Part of the value of self-publishing is the potential for a quick turnaround from concept to finished product. Don't waste valuable time hunting for resources or writing without the roadmap of an outline. We will discuss this topic in more detail later in the book.

Sustainable positive attitude. It is easy to be enthusiastic about a project in the beginning. Fresh ideas often create a natural momentum that can fuel you, making the first part of a project seem effortless. The test comes when that initial euphoria fades and your manuscript is only half finished. At this point you need to nurture your will to finish the project. One way to keep yourself motivated is to make a list of how you will benefit from your project. Are you looking forward to seeing your name on the cover of a real book? Are you writing something that has the potential to help a lot of people? Are you hoping to use your book as evidence of your expertise in a field where you need to generate more business? Keeping your mission fresh in your mind can invigorate your desire to complete your book project.

Humility and eagerness to learn. Confidence in your ability to succeed is one thing; arrogance is another. If you want to make it through this process you have to have an open mind to the ideas of others and the willingness to learn about new processes. One of the best things I did before I wrote my first book was enroll in a course at a local community college to learn more about word processing and document design. I also sought the advice of other authors in my field. One person even agreed to mentor me through my first few writing projects.

Realistic expectations. There is no such thing as perfection. No matter how much work you put into your book, there is always more you can do. At some point you need to stop, praise yourself for finishing the project and move on. The beauty of self-publishing is that you can print a limited edition, review this first printing, and make modifications in time for your second printing.

Assembling Your Dream Team

By now you should have a feel for what you can do for yourself and which tasks you will need help with. In some cases you may have the skills, but you need to conserve your time to write. Some key people to consider hiring include:

- **A developmental editor.** Usually consulted before you begin your project, developmental editors can help plan the structure of your work from outlining to reworking content to improve flow.

- **A page designer.** Usually proficient in advanced publishing programs such as Quark, Photoshop, and

Microsoft Publisher, page designers are experts in page layouts including headings, illustrations, tables, etc.

- **An illustrator or photo editor.** Photographs and other illustrations can be very expensive to purchase, but making an investment in one or two professional graphics, especially for your cover, can transform an everyday manuscript into a competitive product.
- **A copyeditor.** An essential member of any publishing team, the copyeditor corrects grammatical errors, sorts out discrepancies in the text, and checks for consistency of writing style and form.

"If you want to be a writer-stop talking about it and sit down and write!"
Jackie Collins

Key Points of Chapter 2

1. **Be sure you have the basic hardware and software, as well as the skills to embark on this journey.** Many software programs have 15 to 30 day trials that you can download from the internet. You may want to brush up on your skills by taking a community college class or doing some online tutorials.
2. **Be honest with yourself about your writing ability.** Ask other people to critique samples of your writing. Solicit the opinion of an editor, a writing coach, or other authors.
3. **Know your personal strengths and weaknesses.** Weaknesses don't have to be deal breakers. By knowing your personal weaknesses you can seek additional training

or solicit the help of others. Authors who are able to put aside their ego and be "coachable" are the most successful in the self-publishing business.

Resources for Chapter 2

The Academic Superstore
www.academicsuperstore.com
Check out the software bargains on this website. All you need is a student ID or proof that you are a teacher or parent of a student. I was able to purchase Adobe Acrobat for one third the retail cost.

MIT OpenCourseWare
www.ocw.mit.edu
Massachusetts Institute of Technology offers hundreds of free college level courses. Writing topics include creative writing, technical communication, web content writing, poetry, and biographical writing.

Writer's Digest
www.writersdigest.com
This is a fantastic free website with a variety of resources for new and established writers. Find information on how to write better, a forum for writers to exchange ideas including a place where writers can critique each other's work.

Writing.com
www.writing.com
You must visit this website to see everything they have to offer. Not only is it rich with resources and creative prompts for writers, you can exchange ideas with other writers, create your own blog and store your manuscripts in an online portfolio.

Part Two:

Writing Deliberately

"I never know what I think about something until I read what I've written on it."

William Faulkner
American author and Nobel Prize winner

3. Defining and Refining Your Idea

"The secret of good writing is to say an old thing in a new way or to say a new thing in an old way."
Richard Harding Davis—American journalist

What Should You Write?

Although most people reading this already have an idea about what type of book they want to write, some of you may be just curious about the process. Coming up with a subject to write about can be a significant task. At the very least you should be wildly passionate about any topic you will be spending a lot of time writing about. I also suggest that if this is your first attempt at authorship, spend your time learning the process of self-publishing, not researching an unfamiliar topic; write what you already know. To clarify what you want to write about, ask yourself these questions:

1. **What is your education and experience?** Think about your degrees and what subjects interested you the most. What types of work experience do you have? What kind of volunteer work have you done? What have you already written about in newsletters, magazines, or for website content?
2. **What are people asking your opinion on?** What are people telling you to write about? The answers to these questions are indications of what others feel are your strengths.
3. **What topics do you find yourself debating in public and in professional circles?** What are current trends in your field? What are your reactions to or opinions of those trends? How you answer these questions reflects what you perceive are your strengths.
4. **What book topics already interest you?** What books have you read in the past year? How often do you read a book and think, "I could have written that!" It is likely that you *could* have written it, could have written it *better*, and *should* write it now.
5. **What knowledge do you have that you would like to pass on to others?** Are you the one person in your family who knows interesting facts about your genealogy? Do you have a unique skill or expertise that could be of great value or interest to others? What lessons have you learned "the hard way"? The easiest way to set your book apart from others in the same category is to offer your story along with the facts. People will be drawn to what you have to say if they believe you have lived it yourself.

Who Are You Writing For?

Have you ever viewed a commercial on television that just didn't make sense? Did you ever wonder why a company would distribute an ad like that when television advertising is so expensive? On the surface it seems like a colossal waste of money and air time.

Please don't be offended, but the reason you didn't "get" that commercial is that it simply wasn't meant for you. Trust me—advertising agencies are not in the business of wasting money. On the contrary, advertisers are actually becoming more refined in persuasion techniques. They have learned that commercials do not have to appeal to the entire population; they just have to communicate the message to the right people—the people that they want to be their customers.

This is a lesson many writers miss. They get so excited about an idea that they want to share it with the whole world. Today, however, the world is a very busy place, and unless you are speaking directly to someone, your message is likely to be lost among the thousands of messages heard every day. You simply cannot write one book for everyone. Just as contemporary advertisers have found, you will be more successful writing for one defined segment of the population. Of course, with the flexibility, low price, and quick turn around of self-publishing, you can retarget and reprint your book, allowing you to sell your work to a completely unique set of customers. That is a much better way to make the most of your time and money.

Creating a Mission Statement and Working Title

After you identify your general topic and target audience, it is important to summarize what you want to write into one or two concise sentences called a mission statement. Taking time to write a mission statement for your book will help focus the rest of your writing and can even form the core of your marketing strategy later on.

To distill everything you want to write about into a couple of sentences, first ask yourself a few pointed questions:

1. **What topic have you chosen for your book?** Yes, we have covered this before, but it is important to identify this in your mission statement.
2. **What are your qualifications to write about this topic?** What, besides being the author of a book, makes you an expert on this topic? Why should people trust that you know what you are writing about?
3. **What will your target audience look like?** Again, you should already have defined this, but take a moment now to get specific enough that you can see the faces of your customers. For example, instead of stating your target audience will be little boys, say little boys ages 5 to 7. Or, if your book is intended for married couples, maybe you can be more specific and target people who have been married more than 25 years.
4. **What do you want your audience to learn from you?** What value will the audience get from your book? Hint: Try to keep this to two or three main points. If you have more you want to teach you can write a second book!

5. **How long do you want your book to be?** If this is your first time publishing a book, I suggest keeping it simple and keeping it short. Book coach Judy Collins sums it up: "Gone are the days of the 260- page book to show you as the expert," she says. "Think 50-100 pages. Your specific audience is busy like you and wants tips and how to's that help them overcome their problem or challenge."

Condense the answers to these questions into one or two sentences and you have a mission statement for your book. Type it up, print it out, and keep it close. You will refer to it often when you write your manuscript, create the cover, and market your product.

"I never know what I think about something until I read what I've written on it."
William Faulkner

At this point, you can try to sum up everything into a working title for your book. Although this may change over time, it provides you with an increasingly concrete vision for your work. Some other things to keep in mind when choosing a title:

1. Shorter titles seem to be popular these days; however in non-fiction it is important for potential buyers to get the point of your book. Be as descriptive as possible.
2. Your title is your calling card for your book. It should be easy to say and memorable.
3. Online book sales reached a mind-blowing $5.5 billion in 2008. In order for people to find your book, your title

and sub-title should include key words that people are likely to use when they search the internet via Google or the other major search engines. (We will discuss other ways to market your book on the web in Chapter 9.)

4. You should include brief phrases that reflect the ideas in your book on the front, but save most of that for the back cover. The cover may attract a buyer, but most book sales are cinched after people read the back.

Key Points for Chapter 3

1. Write what you know, what you want to be known for, and what you are passionate about.
2. Define your target audience and focus your book accordingly.
3. Create a tightly worded mission statement that reflects your topic, your audience, and the ideas that will be covered in your book. Refer to it often
4. Sketch out a working title based on your mission statement. Be descriptive and use words that potential buyers would use as keywords on a search engine. A successful self-publisher carefully leverages their presence on the internet to improve sales.

4. Organizing Your Writing

"First comes thought; then organization of that thought into ideas and plans; then transformation of those plans into reality. The beginning, as you will observe, is in your imagination."
Napoleon Hill—Author of *Think and Grow Rich*

Controlling the Chaos

I know this is titled Chapter 4, but would you ever guess that this was the first chapter I actually *wrote* for the book? Of course, it isn't the first thing I *did*. I had already sketched out the table of contents, written notes, and created computer files for the other chapters. I had scoured the internet for some inspirational quotes to use and gathered stacks of references. But, this is truly the first chapter I sat down to write.

Very few authors, in fact, would tell you that they sit down to write a book from cover to cover. Sometimes it is a matter of inspiration—you want to write what you are feeling passionate about at the moment. Sometimes it is a matter of time—it is easier to fit writing the dedication into a spare thirty minutes than start a new chapter. Or maybe, you have a slight case of writer's block and you know if you step away from the text to work on the cover or copyright page, it will free your brain to get back to the work of writing. For me, I knew writing the chapter on organization would psychologically settle me in to write the rest of the book more methodically.

Capturing Your Thoughts

Have you ever drawn a blank trying to remember a name or a fact only to have the answer come in a flash hours later? The same can happen when you are writing a book. Once you determine the vision for your book, ideas will percolate easier and will certainly come to you at some of the most inopportune times. The last thing you want is to forget these great ideas because you didn't catalogue them in some way.

Some of you may already have a personal system of organization, but for those who need some additional coaching, here are some suggestions:

1. **Keep a small notebook (or multiple notebooks in various locations) with you, even beside your bed.** You want to capture those tidbits of inspiration whether they occur in the car, waiting in line at the store, or in the middle of the night. Some of the best ideas I have had were written on napkins at restaurants or on the back of church bulletins.

2. **Write down everything that comes to mind**—good ideas or bad. Just get them documented. You can sort them out later.
3. **Use technology to record thoughts**. Don't have paper and/or a pen? Send yourself a voice mail or text message. If you are searching the internet and come across something that you would like to include, email the link to yourself. [I use a uniquely created and dedicated Gmail (www.gmail.com) account for each writing project.] Don't forget to write these ideas down in a more permanent spot as soon as you can!
4. **Capture what you write on the internet.** Participate in online message boards or use a web log (blog) to write bits and pieces of the book. (Free blogs are available from many sources. I have found www.blogspot.com very easy to use.) Writing a newsletter or e-newsletter can serve the same purpose.
5. **Keep a box or file cabinet to store hard copies of ideas**. It may seem like a crude system, but it works. In preparation for writing this book, I gathered all of the books and magazine articles I had collected and piled them into a simple banker's box. Now that box is right beside me as I work on this book.

Setting Up Functional Files

The next step in writing a book is to get all of those brilliant ideas organized in some fashion. Keep in mind, unless you have been good about transferring all of the ideas that you wrote on paper onto the computer, you will likely have some hybrid of paper copy organization and electronic files.

Remember, *how* you organize and file the main topics of your book isn't as important as actually doing it.

Since eventually the company printing your book will need the final document in electronic form as a word processing or PDF file, it is important for everyone to start with computer files. This organization will be critical to streamline the publishing process later on.

In the case of *You CAN Write a Book,* I sketched out a table of contents first, and then created electronic file folders on my computer to reflect the chapters and other major segments of the book (see Example 1). Notice that the name of each file folder begins with a number that doesn't necessarily correspond to the chapter number, but does help keep the files in the correct order. For example, folders 03, 04, and 05 were combined to form Chapter 1, and this chapter is number four, despite the fact that the file folder starts with 08.

Each of the folders contains the primary MSWord documents of the chapter as well as any electronic information that supports the individual topics. Again, don't worry if the chapters change somewhat during the writing process; that happens. Just be sure to create new folders and rename them to keep you organized!

Next, you will need to create some sort of external filing system to organize all of the information that isn't already on your computer. Depending on the type and number of references, you can use anything from a portable accordion file folder to several banker's boxes or crates. The key is to label the individual files the same as your computer files.

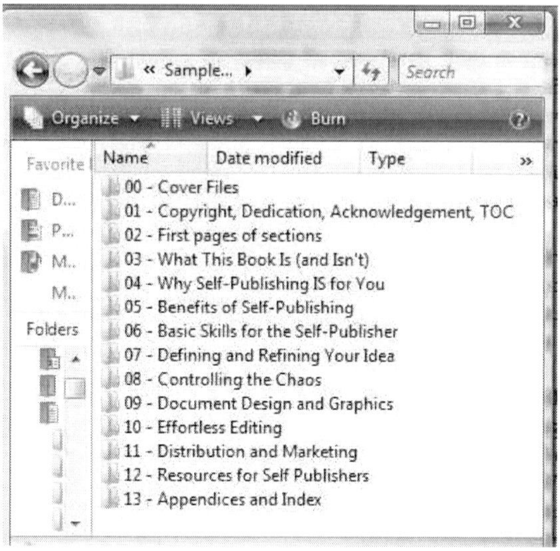

Example 1: Sample Book File Organization.
Notice the numbering in the chapters' folder names to keep files in order.

Finally, take all of your papers, books, magazines, and electronic documents and file them appropriately. Put the hard copies in the boxes or file folder. Sort any electronic documents into the corresponding electronic chapter folders. You can even save internet pages in your electronic folders. Just go to the top of your browser page and click on "File" then "Save" or "Save As," choosing the correct file to save the webpage to.

When it is time to write each chapter, all you have to do is open the corresponding computer file folder and pull the matching material from your boxes or file folders. Using word processing software such as MSWord, start a document for each chapter or section, roughly outlining the chapter with your collection of ideas. (See Chapter 5 for more information on templates and formatting.) It is important to create a different document for each chapter or section right from the beginning because documents larger than 100 pages tend to get corrupted in word processing programs. It also makes editing easier.

Some people regard discipline as a chore.
For me, it is a kind of order that sets me free to fly.
Julie Andrews

Getting the Job Done

Once you have sketched out your chapters, you can begin the exciting task of writing. Here are some hints to make that process as easy as possible:

1. **Establish a place to write.** Your office may or may not be the perfect place. In fact, if you have a laptop, you can write any place that supports your motivation and creativity.
2. **Just Write.** If you have followed the steps so far, you have created a solid working structure for your book. Now, put aside all ideas of perfect writing. At this point no one cares if it is the lousiest writing you have ever done. It can be very seductive to spend valuable time editing and tweaking your work before you have finished writing. You may rationalize that you are working on your book, when in fact, it is just one more way for you to avoid the actual writing. Trust me on this. Set a timer for 30 minutes and get going. I bet you can pour out 5 to 7 pages if you quit worrying about perfection. Then set the timer for another 30 minutes. Repeat as necessary. Before you know it you will have a book.

3. **Balance your need to feel creative with the reality of setting milestones.** Tapping into bursts of creativity can be exhilarating, but don't underestimate the power of setting achievable goals.
4. **Make writing a priority.** Schedule writing into your day. If you already have a full schedule, you may need to temporarily sacrifice other activities. Depending on when you do the best work, wake up 30 minutes earlier each morning, use your lunch hour, or turn off the TV to work toward your goals.
5. **Keep an "after book" to-do list.** Procrastination comes in many forms; in the middle of the writing process, other tasks can suddenly seem more important than they really are at the time. Instead of dodging the writing you know you want to do, keep track of these extra chores, promising yourself you will get to them as soon as you are finished with the book.
6. **Minimize distractions.** Some of the biggest time wasters are email and social networking sites. Make it a rule to check your email only twice a day; and if you find yourself distracted in other ways on the internet, set a timer and stick to the time limit you set.
7. **Create your own deadlines.** Without timeline pressure from a publisher, it can be easy to put off writing. Minimize this tendency by scheduling an event where you will sell or showcase your book. Or, consider selling pre-published copies.
8. **Hire a writing coach or virtual assistant to keep you on track with your writing.** Being accountable to another person can streamline the process. You can also ask a good friend or family member to hold you responsible for your deadlines.

9. **Understand how stress can work FOR (and against) you.** We all know that too much stress can be harmful, but we may overlook the benefits to our productivity. For example, the stress of facing a deadline can trigger your mind to filter out distractions and sharpen your instincts. To avoid the paralysis of too much stress, remember that balance is important.
10. **When finished writing for the day, make a list of what part of the book you will work on next.** Having a task list ready to go can make it easier to sit down at the computer and begin again.

"I don't wait for moods. You accomplish nothing if you do that. Your mind must know it has got to get down to work."
Pearl S. Buck

Some Final Thoughts

SAVE your work FREQUENTLY when writing on your computer. It is one of the most fundamental rules when writing with a computer. There is nothing as maddening as losing entire paragraphs, chapters, and even a whole book of your writing to whatever demon chooses to inhabit your computer on a given day. I have lost work due to power outages, hard drive failures, and even cats knocking my laptop to the floor. One writer I know was devastated to learn that her life's work was wiped out when Hurricane Katrina destroyed her home.

You can't save your work often enough or to more places. Save your work frequently to more than one storage media. Save it to your laptop, burn copies to a CD/DVD, plug in a USB drive, back-up with an external hard drive.

Of course, any back up is worthless if it is all destroyed by a natural disaster or if a thief takes your briefcase with your laptop and all the storage media, too! Therefore, some sort of online backup service can be a priceless investment. You can search the internet for a service that meets your needs. Alternately, occasionally email copies of your draft and other files to yourself for retrieval at a later date if necessary.

Key Points of Chapter 4

1. The fundamentals of organization are the same whether you are a naturally tidy person, or someone who files things in piles. Your goal is to be able to quickly locate all of the resources and references that you need for any particular segment of your writing project.
2. Keep your thoughts and ideas systematically filed in both paper and electronic form, using notebooks, voice mail, text messaging, and even email accounts to stay organized.
3. Establish a place and time to write. Choose a place that maximizes creativity but minimizes distractions.
4. SAVE, save, save your work, and then save it again!

Resources for Chapter 4

Books

Getting Things Done: The Art of Stress-Free Productivity
By David Allen
Allen takes the reader beyond DayTimers and Franklin planners to a proven system of organizing that translates well into book writing and publishing.

Online Back-Up Companies

Carbonite (www.carbonite.com)
SOS Online Backup (www.sosonlinebackup.com)
Norton 360 (www.symantec.com)

Websites

Writers Market
www.writersmarket.com
A fantastic for-pay resource that calls itself the internet's most comprehensive guide to getting published. Includes market listings, contacts, follow-up tools for manuscript subscriptions, storage for manuscripts and submission attempts, and message board system for members.

5. Editing Like a Professional

"I have never thought of myself as a good writer. Anyone who wants reassurance of that should read one of my first drafts. But I'm one of the world's greatest rewriters."
James A. Michener—American author

Dropping the Ego

In Chapter 2 we discussed that humility and an eagerness to learn are important personal characteristics for a self-publisher. In reality, this is true of anyone who wants to publish a book. At some point, someone must look at your work and help you polish it up.

Of course, *you* have to be open to that feedback. I know what some of you are thinking. You are not so sure you want your words torn apart by someone else. It is your baby, after all.
If that describes you, then stop reading right now and gather up four or five books. Check out the copyright page, dedications, and acknowledgements. What you will notice is that every single

book has an editor and more likely a team of editors. Realizing this fact was my editing epiphany. Every one of my favorite authors—J.K. Rowling, Mitch Albom, Fern Michaels, Jodi Picoult, and Nicholas Sparks—had editors. If they could bite the bullet and turn their work over to others, I could too.

Self-Editing Tips for Authors

At this point you may be thinking, "I am not one of those famous writers. How much does editing cost?" You don't need to worry. Remember, one of the key objectives of *You CAN Write a Book* is to show you ways to minimize the costs of publishing your book while still producing a quality product.

In fact, the best way to save money on editing when you self-publish is to do some initial editing yourself. Edit your writing first using these tips, and you will likely pay less for a professional to polish the finished product:

1. **Make sure the first sentence and paragraph of each chapter will capture your reader's attention.** Your book is only as good as the number of pages someone actually reads. A dull introduction or choppiness to the flow of information subconsciously cues your reader to put the book down and take a break, maybe permanently.
2. **Ensure that your book (even non-fiction work) tells a story.** Readers should be able to identify a beginning, middle, and end. Try to create a relationship with your readers and, more importantly, don't patronize them. Balance instructional language or description of complicated topics with encouraging words. Readers should be able to envision themselves successfully executing what you are teaching.

3. **Check your spelling and grammar periodically as you write.** Look for the spelling checker icon on your Word toolbar, or go to Tools > Spelling and Grammar to run a check. You can even tailor the grammar checking function to analyze your writing for passive phrases, possessives, gender agreement, etc. Simply go to Tools > Options > Spelling & Grammar > Settings then choose the items you would like checked by the program. This tool also assesses readability and grade level. (Unless you are writing a technical manual or textbook, most non-fiction books read better at a eighth or ninth grade level.) **Note:** Spelling and grammar checkers are not foolproof. This should be considered a screening of your work, not a final check.
4. **Proofread a printed copy of your formatted manuscript.** Printing a large document at home can be expensive so to save money, you might want to have the manuscript printed at a local copy center like FedEx Office℠ or OfficeMax™. They can also print your book on both sides of the paper to give you a feel for how it will look when printed in a book. Page through it first to check for aesthetic appeal; then read it from front to back.
5. **Ask friends, colleagues, or family to review the printed copy of your manuscript.** This was hard for me at first; I was a bit timid about sharing my unfinished work with my family. I didn't have to worry. Their comments were gently worded and constructive, and my husband's super critical eye and my daughter's English degree have been (literally) priceless additions to my editing "team."

6. **Invite other subject matter experts (SMEs) to evaluate your work.** Many people will gladly fact check your work free of charge if you offer to quote them in your book, promote their business, or acknowledge them as an expert in the field. Be sure to give them an autographed copy of book when you are done!

Finally, the most important thing you can do if you are editing your own work is to put it away for a week. Two weeks would be even better. You really need to clear your head of what you "know" you were trying to say so that you can "see" what you actually wrote! At this stage, you will be reading the book almost as if you were a new reader. It will be easier to spot typos and grammatical errors, and you will be able to assess the rhythm of the book.

Using Professionals to Fine-Tune Your Work

Once your book is in respectable shape, you can turn it over to a professional editor. Keep in mind, the more you do yourself, the less work you will have pay an editor to do.

Finding an editor is easy in an electronically connected world. Many online communities that cater to writers have forums for people to solicit editors. Social networking sites like LinkedIn and Facebook can also provide leads for editors. I have found my editors through personal contacts. A colleague and friend edited this book, and a graduate school classmate edited my first book. The latter is also a graphics artist whose talents came in handy when I was working on a cookbook.

In spite of everything you do, your finished product may still have errors. This is when you must keep things in perspective. Books printed by traditional publishers are sent to market with mistakes all the time. When I was in graduate school, I paid hundreds of dollars for books that had errors in them. The last novel I read had the word "the" repeated in one sentence, clearly a typo that was missed by the *seven* professional editors mentioned in the front of the book. And, each of my books has had errors that I corrected for the second and third printings.

The philosophy that evolved from all of these observations was that every book I publish would be a "living document" under continuous improvement. That is why I will continue to self-publish. It is much easier to correct and reprint your work than it would be if I were working with a traditional publisher.

Key Points of Chapter 5

1. Eventually, all writers need to put their egos aside and let other people review their work. Even authors of best-sellers have editors.
2. Edit as you write. Screen your work using the spelling and grammar checker available on most word processing programs, but review your work carefully after initial screening.
3. Proofread a printed copy of your work to check for errors not easily seen when viewing on a computer screen.
4. Ask friends, family members, and SMEs to review your work.
5. Use professional editors to fine-tune the final product.

Resources for Chapter 5

Books:

Merriam-Webster's Manual for Writers & Editors
From the editors of *Merriam-Webster's Collegiate Dictionary*
A clear, authoritative guide to effective writing and publishing

Write It Right: The Ground Rules® for Self-Editing Like the Pros
By Dawn Josephson and Lauren Hidden
This book simplifies the challenging self-editing process by breaking it down into five easy steps. It is the perfect reference tool for anyone who wants to improve their writing.

Writing Down the Bones: Freeing the Writer Within
By Natalie Goldberg
Learn how to turn ho-hum writing into sweet flowing prose. Goldberg slowly helps you discover the uniqueness of your writing, teaching not just sentence structure but confident creativity.

Websites:

Bartleby
www.bartleby.com/
This site is great if you need a quote or if you want free access to dictionaries, encyclopedias, thesauri, and other reference books.

Merriam-Webster Online

www.merriam-webster.com/

Merriam Webster is the perfect place to look up words and find information. The site offers a dictionary, thesaurus, encyclopedia, podcasts, word games, and many other things that would be of interest to writers and word-lovers.

The OWL

http://owl.english.purdue.edu/

Purdue University's Online Writing Lab (OWL) is an easy to access and easy to navigate website you can use when you are wondering about the minutiae of proper grammar.

SparkNotes Ultimate Style

http://www.sparknotes.com/writing/style/

The web's ultimate guide to grammar provides a searchable database of topics and an easy-to-search A-Z list of common questions.

Also see:

WritersDigest.com

www.writersdigest.com

Writing.com

www.writing.com

6. Basic Document Design

"Nothing you write, if you hope to be good,
will ever come out as you first hoped."
Lillian Hellman

Essential Elements and Layout

How many books have you read in your lifetime? Hundreds? Thousands? Have you ever paid attention to what publishers call the “front matter” and “back matter”? I know I never did until I wrote my first book. Now, I will never take copyright pages, dedications, forwards, table of contents, and appendices for granted again. I am always curious to see what other authors do, who they thank, and how they lay out these book elements.

Take some time to look at the “front matter” and “back matter” of a few books. Which elements are common to all books, and which elements seem to be optional? Do you like how the table of contents is laid out? Who did the authors thank in the acknowledgements and why? What types of books have an appendix or index? Which of these elements are included in a book like yours? If you aren't sure, visit a bookstore or library and check out the competition.

You may notice that the various elements of front matter and back matter appear in pretty much the same order regardless of the book. Here is a description of the various elements and the order in which they should appear in your book. The left or right side of the book is also indicated:

1. (Left) **The inside of the front cover** is usually left blank.
2. (Right) **A Testimonial or promotional page** is optional, but if included is often the first printed page. The back of this page is left blank. Note that although the blank pages are considered within the pagination, they do not have page numbers or headers.
3. (Right) **The title page** is a modified form of the front cover and includes the title, author(s), and the publisher's name and logo. Names of illustrators, editors, and other contributors may also appear here.
4. (Left) **The copyright page** is always printed on the back of the title page. This page includes the copyright notice, printing history, the Library of Congress Catalog number, ISBN, publisher name and address. Any disclaimers or claims of trademark will also usually appear on this page.
5. (Right) **The dedication page** (optional) can be a creative spot in your book. There is no convention for dedication pages. You can dedicate your book to a specific person, to groups of people (i.e. American soldiers), or to your dog if you like.

6. (Left or next right depending on preference) **The table of contents (TOC)** should provide an outline of the books chapters. You may or may not want to include summaries of the chapters in this list. Since the TOC for this book is two pages long, I started it on the left so that the full TOC could be viewed without turning pages.
7. (Left) If the TOC doesn't run over onto this page, it is usually left **blank**.
8. (Right) After the TOC or blank page, you can have pages for **acknowledgements, a preface, and/or an introduction**. These are all optional. Convention states that the back of each of these pages (on the left) is **blank**.
9. (Right) **The first chapter** *always* starts on a right hand page. You may want to follow this pattern for all chapters, leaving some left hand pages blank; however, many books today have the chapters printed one after another without the blank pages between. The first page of each chapter is similar in format throughout the book and includes the chapter number and name, and may include a list of topics covered in the chapter.
10. (Right) **The back matter** can contain any of these elements, but if used are usually placed in the following order:
    a. **End notes.** A list of parenthetical references.
    b. **Appendices.** Important information that was either too long to put directly in the text or serves a supporting purpose. One of the appendices in this book is "Common Keyboard Shortcuts." This information is great to know, but it would have been cumbersome to include in the body of the book.

c. **Glossary.** A short dictionary that defines unusual or unique words used in your text. You may want to include this if you suspect potential readers are not familiar with your topic's vocabulary.
d. **Bibliography.** A list of reference material you used to write your book.
e. **References.** Additional material on your topic, usually books or articles that your readers may find interesting.
f. **Index.** An alphabetical list of words and terms used in your book to make searching for topics easier. Although it is a tedious process, you can create your own index; however, you can also contract this task out with an indexing editor or technical writer.

11. (Right) **Optional elements** in the back of the book include **an order form** for the book and synopses of other books you have written.

Formatting Hints

Document design can be fun IF you have the skills and experience to do it right. At the very least, you should know how to:

- Use templates and set margins
- Change fonts, font sizes, and line spacing
- Create and format tables and text boxes
- Insert photographs and other graphics

If you don't have the skills and experience, and you are in a hurry to get your book printed, do yourself a favor. Hire a technical writer, a virtual assistant, or even a graphics arts student to do it for you. If you are not on a deadline and would like to learn more about document design, you can take a class from a local community college or find an online tutorial. Authors who plan to write more than one book would definitely benefit from taking a class to learn how to leverage the "hidden talents" of Microsoft Word.

Whether you do the work yourself or hire it out, you should know a few simple rules:

1. **Serif and sans serif fonts each have their place.** Fonts can be categorized as either "serif" or sans serif." Serifs are the little hooks that you see on some letters such as the Georgia font you are reading right now. Serif fonts are good for longer text such as the body of a book. Examples of serif fonts include:
    - Times New Roman
    - Georgia (used in this book)
    - Garamond

   Sans serif fonts are best for headings, titles, captions for illustrations and other short passages like the back cover of a book. Examples of sans serif fonts include:
    - Arial
    - Tahoma
    - Verdana
    - Microsoft Sans Serif (used in this book)

   When in doubt keep it simple. Choose one font for your text and one font for your headings. You may want to choose a fancier font for the title of your book.
2. **Font size should be set between 11 and 13 pt.** This is considered the most readable size. Headers and titles can be larger font. Tables and captions for illustrations can be smaller.

3. **The space between lines of words should be larger than single spacing and smaller than double to make the text more readable.** To change the line spacing in a Word document, click on Format > Paragraph > Line Spacing. You may want to play around with the options. I set the spacing between lines in this book to be 16 pt. This is what the text would look like if it were single spaced:

The space between lines of words should be larger than single spacing and smaller than double to make the text more readable. To change the line spacing go to Format > Paragraph > Line Spacing. You may want to play around with the options. I set the spacing between lines in this book to be 16 pt.

As you can see, it really makes a difference!

Inexpensive Graphics

Nothing is more boring that text, text, text. One way or another you need to break the monotony. Judicious use of tables, text boxes, and illustrations can help you accomplish this goal.

The cost of custom art can be quite expensive; still there are some inexpensive ways to acquire beautiful photographs or quirky graphics for your book. Keep in mind that having color pages in your book will significantly raise the cost of printing; so using black and white or grayscale graphics would be wise, unless you are publishing a photography book or a cookbook.

Microsoft Word includes a free picture gallery that includes both photographs and clipart. You may want to look at other books to see what types of graphics are used. I used Microsoft clipart for the images of a flash drive, a CD, and an external hard drive. It was just enough to break up that long block of text, and it served to illustrate the objects I was describing.

Other inexpensive sources for art include Jupiter Images (www.jupiterimages.com) and IStockPhoto (www.istockphoto.com). Both have a variety of packages to choose from, or you can purchase one photo at a time. I have used IStockPhoto for all of my covers so far. I also use IStockPhoto to find pictures for my website and newsletter. At the time this book was printed, IStockPhoto had a fairly liberal use policy for small businesses. However, it is always important to read the Content License Agreements of companies completely before you purchase anything. When in doubt, have an attorney double check it for you.

Finally, on the topic of free or nearly free graphics, you can always ask a friend or family member to take photographs or create illustrations for you. Or you could solicit help from a college art or photography student. Although I haven't met a student yet who would turn down extra cash, you may find a student who would simply be thrilled to see their name among the artists' credits in your book.

And then again, in the spirit of self-publishing, you could always do it yourself!

Front Cover Design

A variety of cover art options exist for the self-publisher. The least expensive way is to do it yourself. If you know how to use tables in Word, have the ability to edit photos and drawings, and have a creative eye, designing an attractive cover can be a fun activity when you are fighting a case of writer's block. There is nothing like seeing a mock up of your "finished" project to kick-start your writing again. Even though I now solicit a lot more feedback than I did in the beginning, I still create the basic covers, print them, and refer to them as I am writing.

If you do decide to design your own cover, you should refer to the Instant Publisher website for a template created exactly for the size of book you are printing. These templates will include margins for "bleeds," or the area where the color goes over the edge during the printing process. (We will discuss the Instant Publisher website in more detail in the next chapter.)

Designing Your Own Cover Art

1. Set up a "table" in Microsoft Word–follow margin guidelines or template provided by printer.
2. Select background color for table.
3. Insert art and text.
4. Recolor sections of the table for eye appeal.

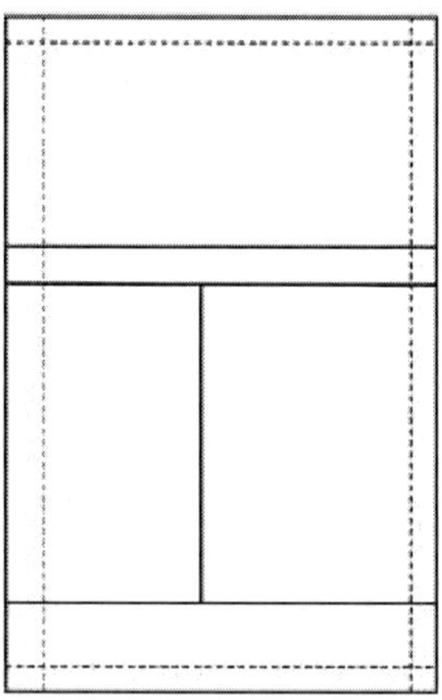

The second option, also inexpensive, is to use a stock cover from Instant Publisher. They have dozens of covers to choose from; however, I only suggest using this option if you are in a pinch or have a very tight budget. The most obvious reason to avoid using a stock cover is that, despite a different title, there is nothing to distinguish your book from others with the same cover. It is also very hard to incorporate other elements of a great cover like words that will attract your target audience and help market your book.

A third option for cover design is to hire an artist. Instant Publisher offers this service for $50 an hour. (They state on their website that 90% of covers can be created in an hour.) Other cover artists can charge $500 to $800 per cover, so this seems like a very reasonable solution for a professional design. Although I haven't used their cover design service, I have paid their artists to tweak my own work.

At this point, you probably know if you have the talent to design the cover of your book. Regardless of the path you choose, as the project manager for your book, you need to understand a few key elements of a great book cover:

Know your target audience. Despite the platitude, "Don't judge a book by its cover," that is exactly what happens. Take a field trip to a local bookstore like Barnes and Noble, get a cup of coffee, and just watch the process people go through before they choose a book. It is almost always the same.

First people look at the cover, and then they turn it over and read the back. If they need more information to make a decision they will open the book and look for testimonials or the table of contents. Although most people will go through all three steps before they buy, the steps usually happen in the same order, and each step is a gateway to the next. In other words, even though people only glance at the front cover, if the title and cover do not click with them right away, they are not likely to take the next important step—turning the book over to read for additional information.

Note that we are talking about the "buyer" here, who may not be the intended reader. Just as you chose your target audience for the body of your book, you need to identify who is actually going to buy your book. Your cover will need to attract both.

For example, the intended audience for your children's book is little girls, ages four to six. You have already written the text and selected internal illustrations accordingly. You would like the cover to be a drawing of two little girls engaged in a tea party. Since most buyers of children's books are parents or grandparents, you might want to show a smiling woman of ambiguous age bringing in cookies and smiling at the scene. A great cover will literally draw the buyer into the creative power of the book, subtly suggesting that the buyer will feel happy about the purchase.

Let's look at another example. If you are writing a book about nurturing a happy marriage, the buyer is most likely to be a woman, even though the content is intended for both husband and wife. Therefore, in order for the book to be available to the husband, a woman has to purchase the book first. Ideally, you should create a cover that appeals to the senses of both the buyer and the other reader.

In this case, imagine a humorous cartoon on the cover illustrating a man and woman tugging on a television remote control. Everyone recognizes this common couple struggle, and it can quickly evoke emotion in both men and women (key to impulse purchases). That picture can even be translated into a clever title like "*It's YOUR Turn to Change the Channel: Seven Ways You Can Make a Difference in Your Marriage.*

Choose font and color deliberately. Naturally, you want a beautiful cover for your book, but you also want to take advantage of every psychological trick you can in order to sell your book. Again, you need to dissect what you like and don't like about other books. For this, you don't have to travel to a bookstore. You can search an online bookstore like Amazon.com. Study the covers of a few New York Times best sellers. What colors and color combinations are currently popular? What types of font and arrangement of text do you see? Make notes about what YOU find appealing. (You can learn more about the meaning of different colors in Appendix C: The Meaning of Color.)

Font styles can also be important. With the number of fonts available in Word, you can probably find something to use that reflects the message you want to communicate. Sans serif fonts are traditionally appropriate for cover text, although you do see quite a few serif fonts on covers today. Try formatting your title using a variety of fonts. The font I used for the cover of this book (Pristina) has a handwritten feel. It is playful without being childish.

If you are looking for something completely different, search the internet for "free fonts," and you will come up with thousands of choices. I recently downloaded a font from 1001 Free Fonts (www.1001freefonts.com) that I will use on the cover of a children's nutrition book. That website allows you to enter sample text to see what the font looks like before you download it. The moment I saw my title in that font, I knew I had a winner!

When placing your title on the cover, be sure to experiment a bit with the location. In most cases, the main title should be slightly above the horizontal center of the book; however, a lot depends on the rest of the cover content. Make the title large enough so that no one has to guess what words designate the title. I came across a book recently with a woman's name in the title. I thought it was the author's name because the font for the title was smaller than the author's name. Unless you are already a celebrity or an accomplished author, keep the title bigger than your name. Other text should be short and to the point.

Testing your cover. When your initial cover design is ready, especially if you design your own, print it on bright white paper using the best printing quality of your printer. You can ask your friends and family for constructive feedback and compare it to the covers of other books written on the same topic. You may be able to get ideas from websites like Writing.com which have forums where authors can share ideas. I posted my cover on an email listserv that I belong to and got great feedback from my colleagues. The cover of this book is not even close to my first few drafts.

You can also upload your cover to Rate My Book Cover (www.ratemybookcover.com). Although the feedback is far from scientific, you can get a feel for how your cover rates against others out there.

Back Cover Design

If you can design a cover that people are attracted to, then the next step is to create the back cover. The back cover of a book is the perfect place for your sales pitch. In a few short sentences or phrases, you need to give the potential buyer every reason to purchase your book.

The text on the back should include a brief description of the book (your mission statement will come in handy here), customer or reader testimonials, and book reviews if you have them. Be sure to include a photo of yourself, a brief rundown of your credentials, and a list of other publications you have written. I have also included my email address and a teaser advertising my speaking services. The ISBN (International Standard Book Number) and EAN (European Article Number) bar code should go in the lower right-hand corner of the back cover. The details of these will be discussed in the next chapter.

Key Points of Chapter 6

1. The front matter and back matter of a book contain specific elements that you should place in a specific order.
2. Convention dictates that certain elements of a book are placed or begin on the left page (i.e. copyright page) and others on the right page (i.e. title page and first page of Chapter 1).
3. For best readability, use a serif font for large blocks of text. Use a sans serif font for headers and other short lines of text. Text size should be between 11 pt. and 13 pt. Space lines larger than single space but smaller than double space.
4. Judicious use of graphics, tables, and text boxes can break the monotony of long text passages. You can get inexpensive or free graphics from a variety of places.
5. Whether you design your cover or not, as a self-publisher you should know how to target your audience, what fonts to choose, and what colors express the emotion you are trying to evoke from a buyer/reader. Be sure to test your cover in a number of ways before you publish.

6. Use your back cover as a place for your sales pitch; include elements of your mission statement. Make a connection with the buyer/reader by putting your picture on the back cover with a list of your credentials, your other publications, and other services.

Resources for Chapter 6

Books

Dynamics in Document Design: Creating Text for Readers
Karen A. Schriver
Based on scientific research about readability and aesthetics, *Dynamics in Document Design* includes guideline on how to create many types of documents including high-tech instruction manuals and textbooks, health communications and information graphics, online information and World Wide Web pages.

Websites

Guerrilla Press
www.guerrilla-press.com
A great resource filled with tidbits about self-publishing. Content includes information on layout, cover design, and descriptions of various bindings.

CafePress Publishing Learning Center
http://www.cafepress.com/cp/info/help/learn_book.aspx
CaféPress has a print-on-demand business, but also has great how-to resources for the self-publisher. Topics include cover design, layout, how to create a PDF file, and how to embed fonts into a PDF file.

Part Three:

Bringing Your Book to Life

"Nothing ever becomes real till it is experienced;
even a proverb is no proverb to you
till your life has illustrated it"

John Keats—English Poet

7. Making Your Book Official

"An intense anticipation itself transforms possibility into reality."
Samuel Smiles—Scottish author

The Requisite Disclaimer

Please remember, I am not an attorney, and I am not qualified in any way to dispense legal advice. The information presented in this chapter (and in the whole book for that matter) is very simplistic and strictly an overview of what can be very complex legal topics. In all cases, I recommend that you consult your personal attorney or an attorney that specializes in publishing law. You should also spend time familiarizing yourself with the various websites mentioned at the end of this chapter to learn more about business structures, ISBNs, copyrights, and trademarks. These websites contain a LOT of valuable information that I can't possibly fit into one chapter of this book.

Setting Up a Publishing Business

Okay, are you ready to make your book "real"? If you plan to sell your book after you publish it, you will need to form a publishing company. In many cases, all you need to do is brainstorm a clever name for your company and apply for a "DBA" license, or "Doing Business As." A DBA is a business name that allows a person to conduct business without having to incorporate or form a unique business entity. In essence, it masks your personal identity, giving your publishing company a name that is different from your own. The bottom line is that your business is still "you." Filing for DBA varies from state to state but is usually inexpensive and easy to implement.

Other forms of business structure like partnerships, limited liability corporations, or C-corporations may be more appropriate for some situations; however, they have more legal and reporting responsibilities attached to running them. To learn more about which business structure will suit you, consult a business attorney and visit the Small Business Advice section of the Small Business Administration (SBA) website (www.sba.gov).

Once you have a business name and structure, it is a good idea to set up a bank account that is separate from your family's account. Since you don't want to print your home address and phone number on the copyright page of your book or on corresponding websites or blogs, consider opening a post office box account and acquiring a toll-free phone number to use for taking book orders. (The toll-free number I have for my business actually forwards to my personal cell phone.) You might even want to design a logo for your business to use on your business cards, book covers, website, and any stationery you use.

The ISBN: A Book's Social Security Number

If you look at the back and on the copyright page of any book, you will see a string of ten or thirteen digits called an International Standard Book Number or ISBN. Just as every person in the United States needs to have a Social Security number, every *book title* that is sold in bookstores or online must have an ISBN assigned to it.

An ISBN identifies both the publisher and one unique edition of a book. Reprints of the same edition will have the same ISBN; however, different versions (for example, hardcover vs. paperback) of the same book will have different ISBNs.

You can only purchase ISBNs from R.R. Bowker, the official ISBN agency for the US (www.isbn.org). Since there is a discount for bulk orders of ISBNs, estimate how many book titles you plan to publish in a five- to seven-year period and order accordingly. At the time of this book's printing, prices were $125 for one ISBN, $275 for ten ISBNs, and $995 for one hundred ISBNs. Once you as the publisher assign one of your ISBNs to a publication, you will log it online with Bowker, and it will appear in "Books in Print," a catalogue and online searchable database used by booksellers and libraries around the world.

A word of caution—it can be tempting to buy your ISBN from sources that offer to "sell" single ISBNs at discounted prices. Please note that these are *unauthorized* re-sellers of ISBNs who are violating the ISBN standards and industry practice. Once the ISBN agency assigns ISBNs to a publisher, that publisher cannot resell, re-assign, transfer, or split its list of ISBNs among other publishers. Thus, owners of these inappropriately reassigned numbers will never actually be the publisher of record for their own books.

I will admit that the one thing that held me back from publishing my first book was the cost of purchasing ISBNs. I knew I would feel obligated to *use* them, and I wasn't convinced that I would write one book, let alone ten or one hundred. What I didn't expect was that the act of ordering those first ten numbers transformed me. I began to *feel* like a publisher, and today, all ten numbers have been assigned to books I have written and books I plan to write.

EAN Barcodes

ISBN: 978-0-9767246-8-1

90000

9 780976 724681

The EAN barcode for *You CAN Write a Book*

Although optional, if you want to sell your books in a retail store you will need a barcode. Instead of the Universal Product Code (UPC) system familiar to most Americans, books use the European Article Number (EAN) barcode system. These EAN barcodes are compatible with systems around the world.

Many companies create barcodes. I order my EAN barcodes from Bowker Barcode (www.bowkerbarcode.com), the same company that assigns the ISBNs. When you order from Bowker, they will send an email that contains your barcode in various file formats. I used the .jpg format and inserted it on the back cover document just as I would any other picture.

Copyrights and Library of Congress

According to the copyright website (www.copyright.gov), copyright is a form of protection provided by the laws of the United States to the authors of "original works of authorship, including literary, dramatic, musical, artistic, and certain other intellectual works." This protection pertains to both published and *unpublished* works. Your work is protected by copyright as soon as you create it. Registration, currently available online for $35, is optional but recommended since a work needs to be registered if you ever need to file a lawsuit for infringement.

When you publish a book, your notice of copyright is placed on the copyright page. A copyright notice consists of:

1. The copyright symbol ©, or the word "Copyright," or the abbreviation "Copr." [You can create the symbol © by typing (c).]
2. The first year that you published the work.
3. The name of the owner of copyright in the work, either your name or the name of your company.

Example: © 2009 Julie Beyer, MA, RD

Finally, if you intend to nurture a brand (such as "Confident Choices®"), or you create a logo for your publishing company, you may need more protection than a copyright. Unlike copyrights which protect entire works, trademarks (symbol TM or ®) protect "distinguishing words, names, symbols, sounds, or colors" from similar items manufactured or sold by others. Although you can apply for a trademark online, applying for a trademark is significantly more complicated than registering a copyright and often requires the advice of an attorney who specializes in intellectual property law.

Key Points of Chapter 7

1. Although you may be able to handle some legal tasks, always seek the counsel of an attorney if you have any legal questions or need help filing applications for business structure, insurance, copyrights, and/or trademarks.
2. It is important to set up a structure for your publishing business. This is required for tax purposes and to protect you, your assets, and your intellectual property.
3. The "Social Security" number for your book is the ISBN. This number is unique to any one version of your book, identifying you or your company as the publisher. Additional printings of identical versions do not need new ISBNs. You can easily purchase ISBNs and the associated EAN barcodes online.
4. Your work is copyrighted the minute you write it. It is, however, inexpensive to register your work with the US Copyright Office, which can mitigate any potential claims.
5. Consider applying for a trademark of your brand name and/or logo to protect the bigger idea of your enterprise.

Resources for Chapter 7

Websites

LegalZoom™
www.legalzoom.com
LegalZoom, an online do-it-yourself legal company offers a comprehensive list of legal services including business formation, trademarks, and copyrights.

Literary Law Guide
http://literarylawguide.com
The Literary Law Guide offers legal resources and copyright information for writers and publishers.

The Publishing Law Center
http://publaw.com
This site provides important legal information for the writing community. Topics include copyright, licenses, trademarks, intellectual property, and contracts.

The Small Business Administration (SBA)
http://sba.gov
Nearly everything you ever wanted to know about running a small business is at this government-sponsored website. Learn how to plan your business, understand pricing of products, and locate small business loans and grants. The SBA website has video and audio tutorials and can direct you to local resources.

The United States Copyright Office
http://www.copyright.gov
Learn more about copyrights and publishing law. Submit your copyright application electronically.

The United States ISBN Agency
http://isbn.org
This website is the only direct source for purchasing ISBN numbers.

The United States Patent and Trademark Office
http://www.uspto.gov
Learn about trademarks and trademark law including proper use of different designations. Applications for trademarks are available on the website.

8. Navigating an Online Publisher

"Any sufficiently advanced technology
is indistinguishable from magic."
Arthur C. Clarke—Science fiction author and inventor

Reviewing Options for Self-Publishing

One thing that distinguishes this book from the 400-page books written about self-publishing is that I overtly favor one method over all the others. The InstantPublisher.com (IP) method is so simple, fast, and inexpensive; I personally don't know why someone would do anything else. And, just to clarify, I am *not* receiving any endorsement money from IP to write this book. I am doing it because I want to teach you what I have learned: Anyone CAN publish a book.

Certainly, there are situations when you might prefer other methods of self-publishing. If you do not want to spend any money on physical books, Print-On-Demand (POD) technology is available and its popularity is slowly growing. With POD, you upload your finished manuscript to a specialized online publisher. The book isn't actually printed until someone orders one. At that point, the POD company prints and ships the book to the customer. There are no boxes in your basement, no packaging to mess with, and no runs to the post office. Although this process meets two of my criteria—it is easy and fast—the disadvantages of this process are *very* real. One, despite the fact you have little or no upfront costs, each individual books costs more to print which can cut into your profit. Two, if you want to take books to sell when you do a talk, or if you want to sell them in brick and mortar stores, you have to buy the books yourself from the POD company. Three, according to some industry experts, the average number of copies sold per POD book is between 75 and 100—again cutting into your potential profits. Most of us want to sell a lot more than 100 books.

Electronically published books or e-books are no doubt becoming a popular option for self-publishers. Several commercial options exist for authors to distribute their books via e-publishing (Amazon's Kindle being only one); however, the easiest way to sell an e-book is from your website. People order. They pay you. You email them a PDF of your book. You are done. As with POD, you don't have boxes or the post office to contend with, and your upfront cost of the books is free with the exception of any software or e-publishing service you may choose to use. Still, many buyers want a physical book either for portability or for convenience. For example, when I write an article or book, I am often referencing other books. I can't imagine having to toggle from one PDF to another on my computer, or bouncing from one book to another on a Kindle. Don't get me wrong, e-books have their place; but we will discuss that in the next chapter.

The InstantPublisher.com Process

That brings us back to InstantPublisher.com. How does their process measure up to my criteria?

- **It is fast.** Turnaround time is about two weeks (three or four for books with color pages). If you need your books sooner, they will rush your order for a fee.
- **It is easy.** All you do is upload your manuscript to their server. They do the rest.
- **It is cheap.** I have looked at other self-publishing options, including other online printers. To date, IP's prices are far lower than their nearest competitor. (The only process that I have found to be cheaper is off-set printing, but that only applies if you buy thousands of books upfront. Although this may be a viable option for you if your book starts to climb the bestseller list, for most of us, the upfront costs are prohibitive.)

Other benefits of IP include their responsive and helpful customer service, access to their in-house graphic artists, the option to order as few as 25 books, their selection of optional marketing packages, and free listing of your book on their website. The biggest benefit to me, however, is their speedy reorder system. All it takes is a couple of clicks and in about two weeks, you have more books!

Pricing. With IP, you don't need to guess or worry about surprise charges when it comes to cost. They have a great tool on their website that tells you exactly what your book will cost (www.instantpublisher.com/pricing.htm). You simply plug in the size of your book, the number of pages, how many copies you want, your binding, and what type of cover you need (white, stock cover, or custom cover). The tool will calculate the cost of each book as well as the cost of the whole order. Take some time to play with this feature. Plug in different scenarios to see what the various options are. What size book is cheapest to print? What if your book has 140 pages instead of 120? What will a hardcover version cost vs. a paperback? What is the cost per book if you order 25, 100, 250, or 1000 copies? (Hint: Although I suggest you try this on your own before you order, in my experience the best price breaks come with orders of 100, 250, and 500.) Although the pricing feature does not show an exact shipping cost, IP only charges you what the shipping company charges them.

Formatting. When you decide what size book you want (5.5 x 8.5 is the most popular), you need to format your manuscript accordingly. You are responsible for making sure your manuscript follows the margin guidelines for the size of book you want to print. You can set the margins of the document yourself, or you can download the corresponding template from the IP website (www.instantpublisher.com/templates.htm). Be sure to refer to the layout suggestions in Chapter 6. For cover templates, see www.instantpublisher.com/covertemplate.asp.

Making PDFs. I personally like to convert my Word files to PDF. I make a separate PDF for each chapter and section of the book and then assemble those into one document. If I decide to make changes later, either to correct typos or add new information, I only need to change one chapter, remake that chapter's PDF, and replace the pages in the main PDF document. Think of it this way. If you take any Word document and add a paragraph in the middle of it, everything after that shifts, sometimes onto the next page. If you have all of your chapters in one Word document, every chapter heading, illustration, table, etc that follows the additional paragraph will be shifted.

Instantly, you have a mess on your hands just because you added a few lines of text in the middle of the book. If instead, you add that paragraph into the chapter, but that chapter is a separate file, you can remake the PDF and insert it without disrupting the rest of the document. Of course, if the additional paragraph pushes the end of the chapter to the next page, you will have to change the page numbers; but that is a small task compared to reediting half of your book!

I use Adobe® Acrobat® to create PDFs. In case you missed it in Chapter 2, I purchased my copy of Acrobat from The Academic Superstore (www.academicsuperstore.com) for about one third of what I would have paid from the Adobe website or an office store. The Academic Superstore requires that you are a student, teacher, or parent of a student to get their discount. I qualified for the discount because my son is still in college. Better yet, you can download a thirty-day trial version of Acrobat from http://www.adobe.com/products/acrobatpro/tryout.html. (At this time, trial software is only available for Windows® users.)

The following steps and suggestions will help you place your first order with InstantPublisher.com:

1. First, sign up as a member to use the IP website. This is free and creates your personal section of the website. You will log in to the member site to upload, store, and reorder your books.
2. If you have a PDF file for your manuscript, you can upload the file directly. If you do not have a PDF file of your manuscript, you will need to install special IP software on your computer to send your document to IP. (Note: This technology is constantly evolving. Please visit the IP site regularly to learn what is new.)

3. Once you upload your document, you will have an opportunity to review it online. **Do NOT skip this important step.** The process of uploading a file can corrupt the document. It is up to you to check your document page by page for errors. Nobody at IP will proofread or edit your book. The file is simply transmitted electronically from your machine to theirs. If the book has errors, they will not be held responsible, unless it is something directly attributable to them.
4. Once you are satisfied with the uploaded version of your document, you can complete the ordering process. You will enter the book size, number of pages, type of binding, and number of books you want to order. Double check your options carefully because once the order is submitted for processing, you cannot change it.
5. As a rule of thumb, you should only order what you are sure you can sell in a year. I usually make my first order small, only 100 or 250 copies, so that I can review the "real" book and make changes if necessary. The fewer copies I print at first, the quicker I can get corrected copies to the market.
6. You will pay half the cost of the order up front and the other half when the books are shipped. Once you receive confirmation that your order has been accepted, you will be asked to email your cover files. Hint: If you order your book with a plastic comb binding, you will need to ask them specifically to print on the spine. They do not do this automatically. If you want to sell your books in stores, you must have the spine printed with the book title and author's name.

7. If you need your books in less than two weeks, you can pay extra for a rush order. Simply notify them by email or phone. Charges for rush orders vary.
8. This is the FUN part! You won't have to just sit back and wait. Once you submit your book, you will see a page in your member section where you can watch the progress of your book. You can see the day your manuscript was accepted, when it is ready to print, when they print it, when they print the cover, and so on.
9. When your book order is completed, you will receive an invoice for the second half of the charges plus shipping. They send you a tracking number that you can use to track your books' journey from the printer to your home or office.
10. Don't hesitate to call or email the good people at IP. I have always found them to be responsive, helpful, and very pleasant to work with. (No, they still aren't paying me to say this, but maybe I should ask them about it! What do you say, IP?)

Key Points of Chapter 8

1. Each method of self-publishing has its own pros and cons. The easiest, quickest and least expensive way (that I have found) to get a "real" book in your hands is to use an online printer like InstantPublisher.com. It is important to do your own research, however, because the business is changing rapidly with evolving technology.

2. To use InstantPublisher.com, you will need to format your manuscript by setting your margins as stated on the IP website or by using the corresponding template. You will also need to format your cover files according to their cover template.
3. Use their pricing feature to get a feel for what your book will cost using different parameters like book size, number ordered, binding, etc.
4. After uploading your manuscript, review it carefully for any errors or corruption that may have occurred during file transfer. If you have problems, contact IP directly. Once the upload is complete, IP will bill you for half the cost up front and half when they ship your order.

Resources for Chapter 8

The Academic Superstore
www.academicsuperstore.com
Check out the software bargains on this website. All you need is a student ID or proof that you are a teacher or parent of a student. I was able to purchase Adobe Acrobat for one-third the retail cost.

InstantPublisher.com
www.instantpublisher.com
IP is one of the least expensive online publishers available. InstantPublisher.com is a subsidiary of FundCraft Publishing, known for publishing cookbooks for fundraising organizations such as schools, churches, and community organizations.

9. Distribution and Marketing

"If you want success, then don't
rely on other people to do what YOU can do!"
Leo Burnett—Advertising executive

Getting Your Book into the Reader's Hands

As many authors have said before me, writing and publishing a book is a lot like having a baby. You work hard for months, writing, preparing, and anticipating. Sometimes the last month is so grueling, you just want the project done so you can see the finished product. The excitement and pride you feel when you crack open that first box of books is incredible. You actually wrote a book! Then, reality sets in and you begin to wonder, "What have I gotten myself in to?"

Hopefully, you took my suggestion and kept your first order small. Unless you have a pre-print order of a thousand books, it is risky to order more than a couple hundred copies until you have your distribution methods in place.

One thing that worries some self-publishers is that they don't have the same access to book distributors as they would when a traditional publishing company prints a book. The truth is that only 30% of books are sold in traditional bookstores anyway, so there is plenty of room for you to get creative when it comes to exposing your book to potential buyers. Here are some ideas:

Amazon.com. Over 20% of books sold come from online stores, and that number grows every year. There are two ways to get your book listed with Amazon.com. You can sign up to have Amazon stock your books and fulfill your orders, or you can sign up to be an independent seller. Of course, it costs more to have Amazon.com hold your inventory and fulfill orders.

Signing up to be an independent seller is actually very easy, and the process of fulfilling orders straightforward. When a buyer orders your book from Amazon.com, Amazon.com collects the money and sends you an email alerting you that you have a sale. You package and ship the books (usually by media mail), and Amazon.com sends you a check about once a month. You can also have the payments directly deposited into your business's bank account. As an independent seller you keep up to 80% of the retail price of your book. You can make a comparison of different selling options by visiting www.amazon.com.

Specialty stores. What is your topic? Are there specialty stores that would provide you with the perfect target audience? Although it might take some legwork, there are probably dozens of niche merchants who would agree to carry a few of your books on consignment or buy books wholesale from you. For example:

- If you wrote a cookbook, you could approach small gourmet food stores.

- If you wrote about your experiences camping, your local RV dealership might be interested in selling your book.
- If you wrote the next great book about cats, check with the local veterinarians or pet supply stores about stocking your book.
- If you wrote a children's book you could sell your book in children's clothing boutiques or resale shops.

I am sure if you brainstorm, you can come up with numerous ideas that fit your topic. What's great about these relationships is that local businesses usually like to support other local businesses. Once you build the relationships, you will likely have some very eager and supportive sales agents on your team.

Presentations. Can your topic be translated into an interesting talk? Approach groups that attract people like your target audience and offer to give a short speech or educational presentation. Ask your friends about the groups that they belong to or check meeting notices in the local paper. Or, if your topic is appropriate, offer to teach a class through your local community education department, making your book a part of the deal. Hint: If you do sell your books when you give a presentation, provide order forms along with your handouts and ask people to volunteer their email addresses. Those who don't purchase your book on the spot may do so weeks later with just a little encouragement.

Organizations and associations. These groups often sell resources to their members via mail order catalogues or their websites. I am currently selling my first two books through two major organizations that specialize in the same topics. These organizations not only buy my books wholesale, they also promote my books in newsletters and other communications with their members.

Inexpensive but Profitable Marketing Techniques

When you think of marketing, you probably envision advertisements in magazines or on websites. Or maybe you see authors appearing on popular talk shows to promote their books. While those methods are good, they aren't always affordable or practical for the average self-publisher. The interesting thing is, it doesn't matter whether you use traditional publishing or self-publishing, the bulk of marketing almost always falls to the author. In fact, many marketing techniques actually work better if you self-publish your book because you have more control.

The theme of your marketing strategy should reflect your target audience and your mission statement. With the glut of communication in today's society, a potential customer may have to see your message dozens (some experts estimate hundreds) of times before they actually buy your book. By targeting your audience with a variety of media and using a consistent message, you can maximize the impact of your efforts.

Therefore, the first step to marketing your book is to rework your core message into a one or two sentence summary. When people ask, "What have you been doing with yourself lately?" you can tell them about your book. The point is to be brief, while still conveying enthusiasm about your project.

For example, the target audience for *You CAN Write a Book* is women ages 25 to 65 who are looking for additional income; and the mission statement is to help these women write and publish their first book using a proven process that is fast, easy, and inexpensive. To capture the attention of my target audience I need to focus my marketing efforts where groups of women gather—church groups, mother's groups, community education classes, and professional association meetings. My core message should consistently reflect the spirit of "fast, easy, and inexpensive." Of course I will use a photo of my book in whatever marketing I do.

Websites. One way or another you need to have a website for your book. The best scenario is to have a domain name (web address) that matches your book title (i.e. www.you-can-write-a-book.com). It is easy to check your "title-as-domain name." Simply type it into a browser, or check with a domain registrar like Register.com (www.register.com) or GoDaddy.com (www.godaddy.com). Be sure to check different variations of the title. I had to put hyphens in the name of this book's website because other versions of the name were taken.

The important thing is that the domain name contains the book's title, which can help raise the webpage in a search engine like Google. Search engines have "bots" that bounce from site to site, logging things like site name, site title, headers, and key words. Although nobody knows exactly how the process works, it is best to use your book title and the key words of your mission statement on your website as many times as possible, without being obnoxious.

In addition to the title, a photo of your book, and links to your Amazon.com page, you might include:

1. Order form and address for mail orders
2. Email and other contact information
3. Author's biography and credentials
4. A calendar of your speaking engagements
5. Testimonials from happy customers
6. Recommendations from colleagues
7. Links to similar associations and organizations
8. A two or three minute video of you doing a sales pitch for your book, or talking about the topic

Both Register.com and GoDaddy.com have web hosting services; however, there are countless options for this. If you don't want to attempt a webpage yourself, you can hire a free-lance web designer. Web designers often work by the hour, so the more you do upfront the better. To save as much money as possible, provide the designer with a drawing of exactly what you expect your website to look like when he or she has completed it.

Website reciprocation. Try to identify companies or organizations that cater to the same target audience as your book and offer to swap "advertisements." If each of you links to the other's website, you both win. Offer to do some writing for their site and ask them to do the same for you. You may also find websites that have online stores where you can sell your book.

Blogs. Weblogs, or simply blogs, are the next best thing to a website. You don't need a web design program to use them, they are easy to set up (try www.blogspot.com), and easy to update. If you haven't written your book yet, a blog is a great way to test your writing. A series of ten substantial blog entries can actually be drafts for ten chapters of your book. With a blog, you can solicit comments. These comments can provide you with valuable feedback when it is time to pull your book together. You may even get some free editing out of it!

Once you have the actual books, you can put purchasing information in your blog. You can also search for other people's blogs that allow open commenting. Although no one appreciates overt advertising, if you can talk about your book's topic, you can also identify yourself as an expert, mentioning your book subtly. This concept of posting comments also works well with Facebook (www.facebook.com), LinkedIn (www.linkedin.com), Twitter (www.twitter.com), and other social networking sites.

Printed materials. Flyers, brochures, bookmarks, and business cards are all inexpensive but effective ways to promote your book. In addition to your name and title, be sure you have your book's picture, the ISBN number, and purchasing information on your printed materials. If you are a speaker, or would be interested in speaking on the topic to groups, mention that also. To keep the cost down, you can design and print these materials yourself, or you can work with the salespeople at your local print shop. Carry your business cards with you wherever you go. You never know when you will run into a potential buyer or meet someone who will ask you to speak on your topic.

Press releases. How do you get totally free, but priceless publicity for your book? You harness the power of the media! But don't just send out a boring press release that says, "Jackie Jacobs just published her new book, *Women of World War II: A Story of Coping, Compassion, and Contribution.* Rather, try to find an interesting angle. For example, in a sluggish economy, many people are planting their own "victory gardens." You can tie your book into this story by letting your local media know you are available to talk to them when they do a story on neighborhood gardens. Better yet, find a great garden yourself to use as an example (reporters love it when you do the legwork). Be sure to couple that great visual with clever sound bites comparing the gardens of WWII with the gardens of today, and you just might get on the news! The important thing is to weave your book and expertise into something else that is intriguing, interesting, or exciting. In his book, *Free Publicity: A TV Reporter Shares the Secrets of Getting Covered on the News*, Jeff Crilley even shows you how to "make" your own news. (By the way, I *highly* recommend his book.)

Using your book to market YOU. Up until now, we have been talking about how you can promote your book. But, what if you turn the tables and have your book promote you? Your book could be one of the best calling cards you will ever have. Being an author can elevate your worth in a potential employer or client's eyes. Think about it. If you had a choice, who would you hire to do a presentation on childhood eating habits—a dietitian, or a dietitian who has written a book about childhood nutrition? All else being equal, you would want the author!

Key Points of Chapter 9

1. Distribution and marketing will likely fall to you as a self-publisher, but if you focus on your target audience and keep your core marketing message based on your mission statement, you can do very well.
2. Make Amazon.com your personal bookstore. Sign up to be an independent seller and keep more of the profit. Ask compatible local businesses to carry your book. Sell your book after you give a talk. Approach organizations and associations to carry and promote your book to their members.
3. Marketing doesn't have to be expensive to be effective. Create an online presence with a website or blog. Reciprocate links with other websites. Use postcards, flyers, and business cards to spread the word. Get creative with the media—the more legwork you do for them; the more they are likely to help you.
4. Don't forget to turn the tables on your book. Not only should you promote your book. You should use your book to promote "you." Everyone loves an author!

Resources for Chapter 9

Books

42 Rules for Driving Success with Books
By Mitchell Levy
A serial entrepreneur shares marketing secrets of successful business people who have used books and authorship as marketing tools to stimulate business growth, establish credibility, and cultivate brand recognition.

Free Publicity: A TV Reporter Shares the Secrets of Getting Covered on the News
By Jeff Crilley
A working journalist shares the secrets of getting covered on the news. Learn how to write press releases that sizzle and fine-tune your story to make the evening news.

Jump Start Your Book Sales: A Money-Making Guide for Authors, Independent Publishers and Small Presses
By Marilyn and Tom Ross
A must have for any small publisher who wants to compete in the big leagues. The Ross' share thousands of ideas from selling your book on the web, how to create buzz, and how to get free publicity.

Websites

BookMarket.com
http://www.bookmarket.com/
John Kremer really does have 1001 ideas for marketing your books. You can also sign up for his terrific e-newsletter.

A Note to My Readers

Before I upload this to InstantPublisher, I have one more thing to say:

If you have something to tell the world, don't wait another day. The world needs to hear from all of you. Your thoughts and stories are far more important than the latest celebrity tell-all. You are the ones living the "real life."

In that spirit, I set up a Facebook group called "You CAN Write a Book." Anyone who purchased this book can join. Let's make this a place where writers can share their ideas, share their progress, and share their success. Who knows, maybe a couple of you can swap editing services!

Oh, and when you finally get your book published, I would like to know. You can email me at NutraConsults@aol.com to send YOUR Amazon.com link. Or, write to me at:

Julie Beyer
NutraConsults
PO Box 210086
Auburn Hills, MI 48321

I really want you to write your book. I want it to be great, and I want it to be a success.

Your cheerleader,

Julie B.

Appendices

Appendix A: Common Keyboard Shortcuts

Shortcuts can make writing easier and more fun. My favorite is Shift F7!

Action	Most Windows	Mac
Undo last action	Ctrl + Z	Cmd + Z
Redo last action	Ctrl + Y	Shift + Cmd + Z
Cut selected text and store on clipboard	Ctrl + X	Cmd + X
Copy selected text and store on clipboard	Ctrl + C	Cmd + C
Paste contents of clipboard at place of cursor	Ctrl + V	Cmd + V
Select all (everything on page or in window)	Ctrl + A	Ctrl + A
Return to start of line	Home	Cmd + ←
Go to end of line	End	Cmd + →
Return to start of document	Ctrl + Home	Home
Go to end of document	Ctrl + End	End
Make bold (or back to regular)	Ctrl + B	Cmd + B
Italics (or back to regular)	Ctrl + I	Cmd + I
Underline (or back to regular)	Ctrl + U	Cmd + U
Make text superscript	Ctrl + Shift + +	Ctrl + Shift + +
Make text subscript	Shift + +	Shift + +
Bring up Thesaurus	Shift + F7	Shift + F7
Copyright symbol ©	(c)	Option-G
Registered trademark ®	(r)	Option-R
Trademark (not registered) ™	(TM)	Option-2

Appendix B: Action Words for Writers

(Source: www.cvisual.com)

abandon	broke	creep	draw
abduct	buck	cripple	dress
abolish	budget	crouch	drill
abscond	built	cut	drink
abuse	bump	dance	drip
accelerate	bury	dart	drop
accuse	bushwhack	dash	drown
achieve	calculate	deal	drug
acquire	catch	decide	dry
act	charge	deck	duel
adapt	chart	deduct	dunk
add	chase	define	ease
address	check	delegate	edge
adjust	choke	delineate	edit
administer	clap	deliver	eject
advance	clash	descend	elevate
advise	classify	describe	elope
aim	climb	design	elude
allocate	clip	detect	emerge
analyze	clutch	determine	endure
answer	coach	develop	engage
anticipate	collapse	devise	enjoin
apprehend	collar	diagnose	ensnare
approach	collect	dictate	enter
appropriate	collide	dig	equip
arbitrate	command	direct	erupt
arrange	commandeer	discard	escape
arrest	communicate	discover	establish
ascertain	compile	display	estimate
assault	complete	dissect	evacuate
assemble	compose	distribute	evade
assess	compute	ditch	evaluate
attack	conduct	dive	evict
attain	conserve	divert	examine
audit	consolidate	do	exert
avert	construct	dodge	exhale
bang	consult	dominate	exit
bar	control	dope	expand
beat	coordinate	douse	expedite
berate	counsel	draft	expel
bite	count	drag	explode
blast	cram	drain	experiment
block	crash	dramatize	explain
blow	crawl	drape	expose
brighten	create	increase	extend

extirpate	gesture	indict	listen
extract	get	induce	log
extricate	give	inflict	lunge
fade	gnaw	influence	lurch
fake	gossip	inform	maim
fall	gouge	inject	maintain
falter	grab	injure	make
fan	grapple	insert	manage
fast	grasp	inspect	mangle
fear	greet	inspire	manipulate
feed	grind	install	march
feel	grip	instigate	mark
fend	gripe	institute	massage
fight	grope	interchange	maul
file	grow	interpret	measure
fill	growl	interview	meddle
finance	grunt	invade	mediate
find	guide	invent	meet
finger	gyrate	inventory	mentor
fix	hack	investigate	mimic
flag	hail	isolate	mingle
flap	hammer	jab	mobilize
flash	handle	jam	mock
flatten	hang	jar	model
flaunt	harass	jeer	molest
flay	haul	jerk	monitor
flee	head	jimmy	motivate
flick	help	jingle	mourn
flinch	hesitate	jolt	move
fling	hide	judge	mumble
flip	hijack	jump	murder
flit	hit	keel	muster
float	hitch	kibitz	mutilate
flog	hobble	kick	nab
flounder	hoist	kidnap	nag
flout	hold	kill	nail
flush	hover	kneel	needle
fly	hug	knife	negotiate
fondle	hurl	lash	nick
force	hurtle	launch	nip
formulate	hypothesize	lead	observe
fornicate	identify	lean	obtain
found	ignore	leap	occupy
fumble	illustrate	learn	offer
furnish	imitate	lecture	officiate
gain	implement	left	operate
gallop	improve	level	order
gather	improvise	lick	organize
generate	inch	limp	oversee

pack	present	reduce	scoot
paddle	presented	reel	score
page	preside	refer	scour
pander	primp	regain	scout
panic	print	rejoin	scrape
parachute	process	relate	scrawl
parade	prod	relax	scream
paralyze	produce	relent	screw
park	program	render	scrub
parry	project	repair	scruff
party	promote	repel	scuffle
pass	prompt	report	sculpt
pat	proofread	represent	scuttle
patrol	propel	repulse	seal
pause	protect	research	search
paw	provide	resign	seduce
peel	provoke	resist	seize
peep	pry	resolve	select
penetrate	publicize	respond	sell
perceive	pull	restore	sense
perform	pummel	retaliate	serve
persuade	pump	retreat	set
photograph	punch	retrieve	sever
pick	purchase	reveal	sew
picket	pursue	review	shake
pile	push	ride	shanghai
pilot	question	rip	shape
pin	quit	rise	sharpen
pinch	race	risk	shave
pirate	raid	rob	shear
pitch	raise	rock	shell
placate	rally	roll	shield
plan	ram	rub	shift
play	ransack	run	shiver
plod	rape	rush	shock
plow	rattle	sail	shoot
plunge	ravage	salute	shorten
pocket	rave	sap	shout
poke	read	save	shove
polish	realize	saw	shovel
pore	receive	scale	show
pose	recline	scamper	shun
pounce	recommend	scan	shut
pout	reconcile	scare	sidestep
pray	reconnoiter	scatter	sigh
predict	record	scavenge	signal
preen	recoup	schedule	sip
prepare	recruit	scold	sit
prescribe	redeem	scoop	size

skid
skim
skip
skirt
slacken
slam
slap
slash
slay
slide
slug
smack
smear
smell
smuggle
snap
snare
snarl
snatch
snicker
sniff
snitch
snoop
snub
snuff
snuggle
soak
sock
soil
solve
spear
spell
spike
spin
splatter
splice
split
spot
spray
spread
spring
sprint
spurn
spy
squeak
stack
stagger
stamp
stand
start
startle
steal
steer
step
stick
stiffen
stifle
stomp
stop
strangle
strap
strike
strip
stroke
struck
stub
study
stuff
stumble
stun
subdue
submerge
submit
suck
summarize
summon
supervise
supply
support
surrender
survey
suspend
swagger
swallow
swap
sway
swear
swerve
swim
swing
swipe
switch
synthesize
systematize
tackle
take
tap
target
taste
taunt
teach
tear
tease
telephone
terrorize
test
thrash
thread
threaten
throw
tickle
tie
tilt
tip
toss
touch
tout
track
train
transcribe
transfer
translate
trap
tread
treat
trip
trot
trounce
try
tuck
tug
tumble
turn
tutor
twist
type
understand
undertake
undo
undress
unfold
unify
unite
untangle
unwind
update
usher
utilize
vacate
vanish
vanquish
vault
vent
violate
wade
walk
wander
ward
watch
wave
wedge
weed
weigh
whack
whip
whirl
whistle
wield
wiggle
withdraw
work
wreck
wrench
wrestle
write
yank
yell
yelp
yield
zap
zip

Appendix C: The Meaning of Colors

Color	Meaning
Red	The color of blood and fire suggests confidence, warmth, love, anger, danger, boldness, excitement, speed, strength, determination, desire, courage, and danger.
Orange	The color of excitement and cheerfulness can also indicate low cost, affordability, enthusiasm, stimulation, and creativity.
Yellow	The color of summer creates feelings of optimism, liveliness, comfort, liveliness, energy, intelligence, happiness, and sometimes danger.
Green	The color of money reflects contemporary values, durability, reliability, environmental issues, optimism, safety nature, calm, relaxation, Spring, safety, honesty, optimism, harmony, and freshness.
Blue	The color or the sky and peace can give the impression of professionalism, loyalty, stability, reliability, and honor, but may project melancholy, boredom, and coldness.
Purple	The color worn by Roman emperors reflects power, royalty, nobility, elegance, sophistication, artificial, luxury, mystery, royalty, fantasy, and magic.
Brown	The color of earth emanates feelings of relaxation, confidence, reassurance, nature, solidity, reliability, genuineness, endurance.
Black	The color often associated with death can also project elegance, sophistication, formality, power, and strength, but also illegality, depression, and immorality.

To order more copies of

You CAN Write a Book

Send cashiers check or money order for $15.00 to:

NutraConsults
PO Box 210086
Auburn Hills, MI 48321

Your Name______________________________

Address______________________________

City, State, Zip______________________________

email______________phone______________

or visit www.you-can-write-a-book.com or www.Amazon.com

To order

Confident Choices:
A Cookbook for Interstitial Cystitis and Overactive Bladder

Send cashiers check or money order for $30..00 to:

NutraConsults
PO Box 210086
Auburn Hills, MI 48321

Your Name____

Address____

City, State, Zip____________________________________

email____________________phone____________________

or visit www.ic-diet.com or www.Amazon.com